EFFECTIVE HUMANITY

CHARU GUPTA

Dedicated to the youth aspiring to be future leaders.

Contents

Foreword

Power is synonymous with leadership. Those desirous of being powerful must pursue effective humanity. Humanity when pursued effectively always leads to empowerment of those being lead. Thus, in turn empowering the leaders to do better for the welfare of humans.

CHAPTER ONE

EFFECTIVE HUMANITY

The real meaning/lesson of divinity is to realise that a human being is the central part of nature and the natural environment. We are the main protagonists of all the actions, events and processes taking place on the earth and even beyond. We, through our karmas, make events occur. Our action is the cause of the resultant effect. The life we are bestowed with is a gift from the divine to empower us to explore the possibilities for a better future/fate. We must use our intelligence for the solutions to existing challenges. We, the humans, can heal any trauma by connecting with nature. We are living and therefore, we should attempt to connect with other existing living beings present in nature. We should ensure our participation and involvement in the pursuits of sustainable development for our future generations. We can gain the tranquillity to lead a normal life and to let the world be a peaceful and harmonious place by following the dharma of doing the just and right karmas. We must maintain our faith in the beliefs contributing to the welfare of humanity and upliftment of humans. Our real connection with God happens when we perform our acts for the benefit of humanity because real spirituality guides us to not interfere or disturb the process of justice i.e. to let life prevail without any harm. The real connection with God and the real godliness lies in the protection of innocent and preservation of innocence in the human psyche. Therefore, let us all decide to be good human beings for the prevalence of effective humanity which is not disturbed by illegitimate trauma and sorrows. This world will be a better place when the interests of living become the foremost priority. If we are more compassionate towards the needs of fellow humans, if we direct our intentions towards humanitarian causes, and if we pay more heed to the resolution of issues that disturb the living beings on earth, we can create a better world for future generations to bloom. And that would be the more befitting contribution to the survival of the human race and also to the survival of other life forms.

The main idea of effective humanity constitutes the expression of compassion towards other humans and all other life forms. Compassion necessarily means to let life exist and to not disturb the balance of energy and matter. In the human realm, it essentially means not causing sorrow to other humans and not disturbing the human psyche with illegitimate threats. We all want to live in a peaceful world with an abundance of natural resources for the sustenance of life in the future and when we direct our karmas towards the same, we can achieve the idea of humanity that is not merely rhetorical but also effective in occurrence. Therefore, the idea of effective humanity can save us from future threats and can also ensure the prevalence of a healthy and compassionate world. *Only compassion can save the human race from illegitimate threats which may disturb their psyche and physical existence for the real power is to be a good human. Innocence is the most prized virtue to be found in a civilized society and an innocent man is the most prized possession of civilized society because he is no threat to the existence of humanity.*

CHAPTER TWO

Humanity is spirituality manifested by practising compassion for the sustenance of life.

Aggression is the enemy of compassion. We should practice compassion while searching for solutions of our problems. Confrontation is easy but discussion for the relevant solutions is what we should do. We are educated and empowered to conduct a healthy dialogue. Correct discussion empowers the concerned persons to reach the correct solution. Whatever may be the issue, a compassionate approach will always render the required appropriateness to the process of reaching the solution. A solution sought for any problem ultimately relates to the problems of humans and all other forms of life. Therefore, the solution must be sought while considering the welfare and upliftment of humans, nature, and other living beings.

Aggression will not do any benefit but rather make matters worse. Therefore, confront if you must, but always for the benefit of living. We must not forget that the life occurring on Earth is the same in every part of the planet. The only difference lies in the environmental conditions and the adaptations of the living according to the environment. Therefore, the loss of innocent life on any part of the earth is equally disturbing for the entire population of humans on the entire earth. Therefore, we must practice compassion to get to the solutions to render more appropriateness to its enforcement and make it realise that empathy will make it easier for humans to survive any calamity. _There is no superior spirituality than practising compassion for the sustenance of humanity._

CHAPTER THREE

Your fate is the fortune acquired by you through your karmas.

Fate is the fortune received when the power of your karmas which are done with legitimate hard-work and pursued in the right direction of dharma i.e. karmas performed with honest intentions result in success. We all want to be powerful. We all seek the power to achieve success. One essential idea to be understood in the process of achieving that power is that being powerful means to realise that the ultimate power in this world is to be a human being. We are the administrators of all the resources of the earth and beyond. The fortune we seek from our fate is nothing but the result of our performed karmas. The better causes we create the better effects we can expect from our actions. The realisation that we can control the events happening on the earth makes this power surreal. This is like a fantasy being manifested. But the results of the events whether good or bad bring us back to the reality that a human is still a very small part of the world. We must maintain our gratitude to the divine for this wonderful system of the natural environment that does not let any deficiency of nourishment affect us, to our family and friends for nurturing us with love to maintain the essential humane qualities in our psyche and to the existence of humanity that has always acted to save us from any threat in any part of the world. When we ensure that our deeds align with the principles of humanity we are contributing to enhance the feeling of amity in the world. Therefore, when we perform our acts with good intentions and for human welfare we can be assured that the results will offer us a fortune that only a man with a good fate is bestowed with and that is very fortunate for humanity. There is no denying that sometimes a human has to undergo a lot of challenges and troubles but the realisation that you can overcome the challenges and overpower the causes of misfortune makes you emerge as a victorious human. Thus, the real power is sought for the most powerful cause of change is a human and the most powerful agent of change is also a human.

CHAPTER FOUR

We can achieve the goal of humanity when the exercised morality results in the sustenance of balance in nature.

A human being requires an optimum balance of conditions in the natural environment to survive. We want clean air, clean water, unadulterated food, clothes suitable to the environmental conditions to maintain the body temperature for the proper functioning of our body, etc. These conditions ensure the survival of the human body. There are other conditions also that make our existence more relevant. Those are education to enhance our intelligence, affection towards other humans to nourish our emotional development, involvement in some task or work to nurture our personalities and engagement in devotion (for some purpose or towards divinity/spirituality or for some goal) to maintain our emotional balance. The era we are presently in requires us to be considerate towards the environment. We must think about adapting our routine activities to achieve the goal of sustainable development. We must ensure the provision of resources for our future generations. Just as we need sustainable development, so is the requirement for the prevalence of good notions, ideas, thoughts, emotions and behaviour in the human realm of the environment. We require a balance of emotions in our minds to conduct our work and behaviour properly. There is a need for human values, such as devotion, affection, wisdom, honesty, concern, compassion and empathy in society, without which a human can not survive even in the most appropriate environmental conditions. *Therefore, we should deliberately exercise and practice the ideas of morality to achieve the goal of humanity for the achievement of balance in nature for the optimum occurrence of all the factors required for the sustenance of life.*

CHAPTER FIVE

The power of goodness supersedes the power of all other qualities.

Opposite to our expectations, we encounter problems due to unavoidable circumstances. The reason for this could be any. We may get stranded in a challenge, problem or trouble. We must maintain inner peace and calm while facing any of these. We must rely on the strength of our personality. The problems should be taken as a test to develop the courage to come to a resolution. No trouble can deter a man who seeks strength from his personality. We should not feel timid while searching for strength from our inner recesses of personality. We all are brave and strong. When we seek strength from our personality, our conscience guides us towards the solution. That solution will be correct because when we have faith in our abilities, we can trust the best creation of the almighty, in which he sees his reflection. Therefore, one should always keep oneself learned and wise to know the difference between right and wrong to comprehend the problem correctly for the right solution.

CHAPTER SIX

The power you want to unleash is directly proportional to the quality of your karmas.

According to the human perception, the most powerful entity in the world is the divine. When we are in trouble, we seek divine guidance and protection. We perceive that divinity can make us come out of it. In our dharma, we can establish our connection to God through understanding the scriptures written about the human incarnation of the divine form. The essential lesson is to follow the dharma of performing the right karmas by staying away from injustice. We should be performing deeds that lead to the protection of the innocent and the preservation of innocence. In the current era of human existence, we can become powerful by performing our deeds with consideration for a better world. The goal of one world, one life - can help us. It means to consider all the life on earth to be equally important. We can not let an innocent life suffer. That would be an injustice. When we work for human welfare and upliftment, we make ourselves powerful. A powerful human is safe anywhere in the world, who can rely on humanity for his safety, who conducts his work with an honest heart, who doesn't hurt anybody and who ensures the survival of humanity.

CHAPTER SEVEN

Anger Footprint

Contradictions over frivolous issues lead to illegitimate confrontations, which threaten humanity. Simply put, it takes less energy to maintain peace and harmony and more anxiety and anguish to get angry. We can reduce the anger footprint by being more positive and honest and less prone to human fallacies. Just as more carbon footprint is dangerous for the physical life, so is more anger footprint for the mental wellness. Let us reduce both.

CHAPTER EIGHT

Access to humanity makes a man powerful.

Humanity means the collective power of the good qualities of humans in the world. Humanity is a positive word. When a human has access to humanity, he has the power of faith with him. He can rely on the power of being human. A human has the power to be affectionate, considerate, honest, just, innocent, faithful, devoted, kind and compassionate. The exertion of all these qualities will make a human the most powerful. That power is 'The Power to Survive'. A human can live most comfortably when he has the power to survive. Thus, when the good qualities of humans are made accessible, it becomes the most comfortable for them. Simply put, power is nothing but humanity realised.

CHAPTER NINE

The Power to Lead.

You can not put confidence in the public by telling them they are weak. But you can always empower them by encouraging them to be strong and when you intend to act an agent to provide that power, you should be a part of the opportunity that will render the status of powerful to them. This century is the century of the status of being POWERFUL. Citizens look up to leaders for power - the power to achieve, the power to be self-sufficient, the power to prosper, the power to be upright and the power to be non-compromising for humanitarian concerns. Let us defend this power. Let us understand the real concerns of the youth of this century and render that power to them - The Power to Lead.

CHAPTER TEN

Life is a gift from the divine.

Life is a gift from the divine
    We are thankful to the Mother Nature
    For this beautiful world
    For diversity in the animal kingdom
    For grey in elephant and gold in lion
    For huge in elephant and bold in lion
    For trumpet in elephant and roar in lion
    For sugarcane for elephant and boar for lion
    We cherish this diversity found in the animal kingdom
    No human can ever be so creative as Mother Nature
    It has been a generous source of nourishment for the
entire range of biodiversity
    And is unparallel in the range of its creativity
    Although we can denote this biodiversity to the
scientific process of evolution
    Yet, no creation is complete without the inclusion
    Of life, to which the God's hand is the only contribution
    Because a body is the work of science
    But the life is the creation of the divine
    We can study the science
    But to understand life is to comprehend the divine

This world is God's canvas,
And he is the best artist
He can breathe life into his creations
Therefore, let us be considerate towards life
And be thankful to the divine
For the beautiful device called the body and its wonderful design.

CHAPTER ELEVEN

Protecting the innocent is a divine obligation.

FIGHT

Fight the pain
that is causing trembling in your mind and body
whatsoever, the cause be
overcome the timidness
that is causing you to suffer and not fight
Fight the fear
get out of the confines of your mind
that tells you to stay fearful
It is your foremost duty to protect yourself
And the only way to do so is to be brave
Fight the crime
that is hurting your mind and soul
For you are no less powerful
you have the power of faith
you have the shelter of God
Overpower the maliciousness
that is causing the crime

Drag the criminal out of the refuge of his nefariousness
and punish the crime
kill the menace
not only for your own good
but for the sake of entire humanity
FIGHT

It is extremely saddening for the humanity when an innocent man suffers. Attacking an honest man's innocence deserves the wrath of the divine. May that wretched soul who tries to crush the innocence be given the strictest punishment. Since this difference between good and bad is created by the divine and we know that the divine is always favouring and helping the innocent. Therefore, no matter how much and for how long the suffering continues, one should never lose hope and keep trying to resist, persist and survive. Always resist the bad and never let it rot or destroy the goodness within you. Goodness and uprightness are the only solutions to remove the bad. Persist through the bad circumstances. Do not yield to the bad. Always maintain strength. It is understandable, that the longer the struggle continues, the more difficult it becomes to survive as it eats up your reserves of bravery and courage. But you should always maintain the optimism and positivity to fight evil because it is not only for your own good but also for future generations to set a precedence that the evil has to bow down to the good. Only good has the power to destroy the evil. Survive at any cost. Do not surrender. When a brave man wins over evil and bad, the world takes notice of the problem. Because only a victim knows the pain of suffering from the menace. Therefore, your victory will be a relief to all other innocents who are undergoing pain due to the same menace.

Let your win speak for the struggle you have overcome. Crush the menace. Free the future generations from the pain of the crime. Let your win heal the wounds of the struggle. Let your fight be etched in your memory to forget the pain of the crime. Let your win take over the long years of struggle and suffering and be an example for the world to take notice of.

Yes, it is difficult. Yes, it is painful. Yes, it is disheartening. But if you could overcome, overpower and win. It is worth it.

Therefore, the bravery of a man who wins over evil is applaudable for the precedence created by him will be a relief for humanity from a painful crime and will serve to protect and preserve the innocence of future generations.

CHAPTER TWELVE

Power is your Right.

Power is your Right
    To do the right
    Power is your duty
    To be performed duly
    Power is to be responsible
    To make everything good possible
    Power means to protect the humanity
    To maintain the necessary amity
    What else do you want to be powerful for?
    There is no better choice than to choose the right
    There is no better karma than to perform your duty
    There is no better responsibility than to be able to do
good for others
    There is no better place than a happy world
    Those who dare to do good are the most brave
    For they are the reason for the happiness of others
    The real meaning of exerting power is to show that
you have chosen the right to perform your duty for the
prevalence of a better world where the happiness of others
is also as important as yours.

CHAPTER THIRTEEN

Fight.

FIGHT
   Overpower all the opposition
   Overcome the defeat
   Conquer the enemy
   Overpower all the opposition
   Fight the resistance
   Overpower those who oppose
   Overcome the blows of the attack
   Resist, Persist and Survive
   Resist the voices that tell you to leave
   Persist through the circumstances that tell you to disbelieve
   Survive the battle at any cost
   Because you are the winner chosen to be of the select lot of those who write the history
   Overcome the defeat
   Remove the option of not acting
   Choose to fight
   Gather your energy
   Act according to your might
   When you opt for the right to win
   All the lethargy dissipates
   And when you act according to your will

All the success prevails
Adorn your soul with the ornaments of courage
Get ready for the feast of victory with the class of rare and vintage
Defeat the enemy
Attack with all your might
Do not yield
Do not surrender
Let the enemy tell the story of his defeat
That to fight with you is a blunder
Let him realise that the will of God is to choose the brave
And there is no option but you who the success will crave
To bestow the crown of victory
To be selected for the throne of ivory.

CHAPTER FOURTEEN

What does a common man of the world desire?

A common man is not weak. The innocence he carries in his heart is his biggest strength. Although, he is not a part of the power circle of big and influential, the innocence in his heart is more desired than any other influence. A government is a system of administration to conduct the affairs of the machinery of governance to provide amenities, services, infrastructure and development to the citizens. We are in the age of democracies where the public is the most powerful. We give power to our leaders for the deliverance of the effective administration i.e. conduct of an effective function of governance for the welfare and upliftment of citizens. Human beings/citizens/public/ common man are the main components in this idea of democracy. We run the government for us and by ourselves. Therefore, the concern for humanity and humanitarian causes is the only criterion for the functioning of this governance. The progress of citizens is the only and most important function of this system of democratically elected governments. Therefore, the leaders who have concern for humanity are the most desirable not only for their own countries but also for the entire world. Because a wound to any human/ torture to any innocent/ crime inflicted on the innocence has no excuse and it affects not only the victim but the pain hurts the entire generation of humans. The psychological effect on other humans is equally devastating. We can't imagine somebody like us getting hurt though living in any part of the world.

Therefore, the biggest lesson for the new generations of leaders is to have the utmost concern for humanity for the entire world. We are all the same having been constituted of the same type of physical and mental structure. And we all want everybody to be happy. Therefore, let us all take a pledge to shun our prejudices and biases and disregard differences in our socio-cultural structure and devote ourselves to the cause of welfare and upliftment of humans and humanity.

We are in the age of global connectivity. The more affectionate we become to other humans, the better world we will leave for our future generations. That will be a world full of respect and regard for humanity and that essentially means a world less affected by devastations, torture, crime and sadness. And a world which is more abundant in devotion, affection, love, compassion, peace, justice and humanity.

9 7 9 8 8 9 4 1 5 1 6 0 1